Progressive Debate

BILAL QURESHI

ACTIVE 2

Preface

The Progressive Debate series consists of a string of articles on a variety of daily life issues in order to offer two-sided perspectives in each unit which can help learners connect their background knowledge to the topic. The most distinguished feature of this book series is the combination of warm up, pre reading and listening, and main comprehension exercises which develop learners' fluency and accuracy. These comprehension exercises allow students to fully grasp the topic in depth through the course of the whole series. The step by step progression of comprehension exercises engages learners to develop their knowledge for a more evocative conversation. These exercises lead students to develop their own unique perspectives about the topics and engage in meaningful conversation as a final goal.

Reading

A variety of daily life topics with lots of interesting and eye catching vocabulary words are one of the best features of this series of books. All articles are followed by a series of exercises that will certainly help learners improve their comprehension skills.

Discussion

Progressive Debate has been specifically designed to target discussion based classes. It further emphasizes students' need for all four components of language including speaking, reading, writing, and listening.

Writing

Through a systematic organization of comprehension exercises, learners are able to produce a well-organized paragraph in written form.

Step-by-step execution plan for Progressive Debate in Classroom

1. Brainstorm about the topic using questions given in the warm-up section.
2. Get ready for reading by completing pre-reading exercises. Match the target words to their synonyms and explore the meaning of useful expressions given in the contents.
3. Read or listen the content and find the main idea.
4. Find the answers to the comprehension questions in each article.
5. Fill in the blanks using the given words.
6. Complete the sentences by matching one from each section in exercise 3.
7. Fill in the blanks and complete the summary of the article. After filling in the blanks, summarize the important points of the whole article orally.
8. Find grammatical errors in sentences and correct them.
9. Engage your group mates in a discussion using the questions given in exercise 6. These questions will help learners develop their own opinions about the topics. Try to ask more follow up questions to explore your peers' opinions.
10. Read the question in exercise 7 carefully and brainstorm for ideas with your peers. Complete the writing task as a homework assignment.

Components

Student book & Online Audio Recordings for each Article.

Key Feature

The Progressive Debate Active series is a three level, speaking oriented series of books for intermediate proficiency level English learners.These books include a series of interesting and relevant daily life topics to help English learners enhance their communication skills by participating in classroom debate. The articles contain a wide range of vocabulary, useful expressions, and step-by-step comprehension exercises to help learners develop their opinions and express their ideas in more logical and fun ways. This book series proves to be the best solution for English learners' fluency development because of its unique organization of exercises that help to develop learners' ability and knowledge gradually.

Progressive Debate

Table of Content

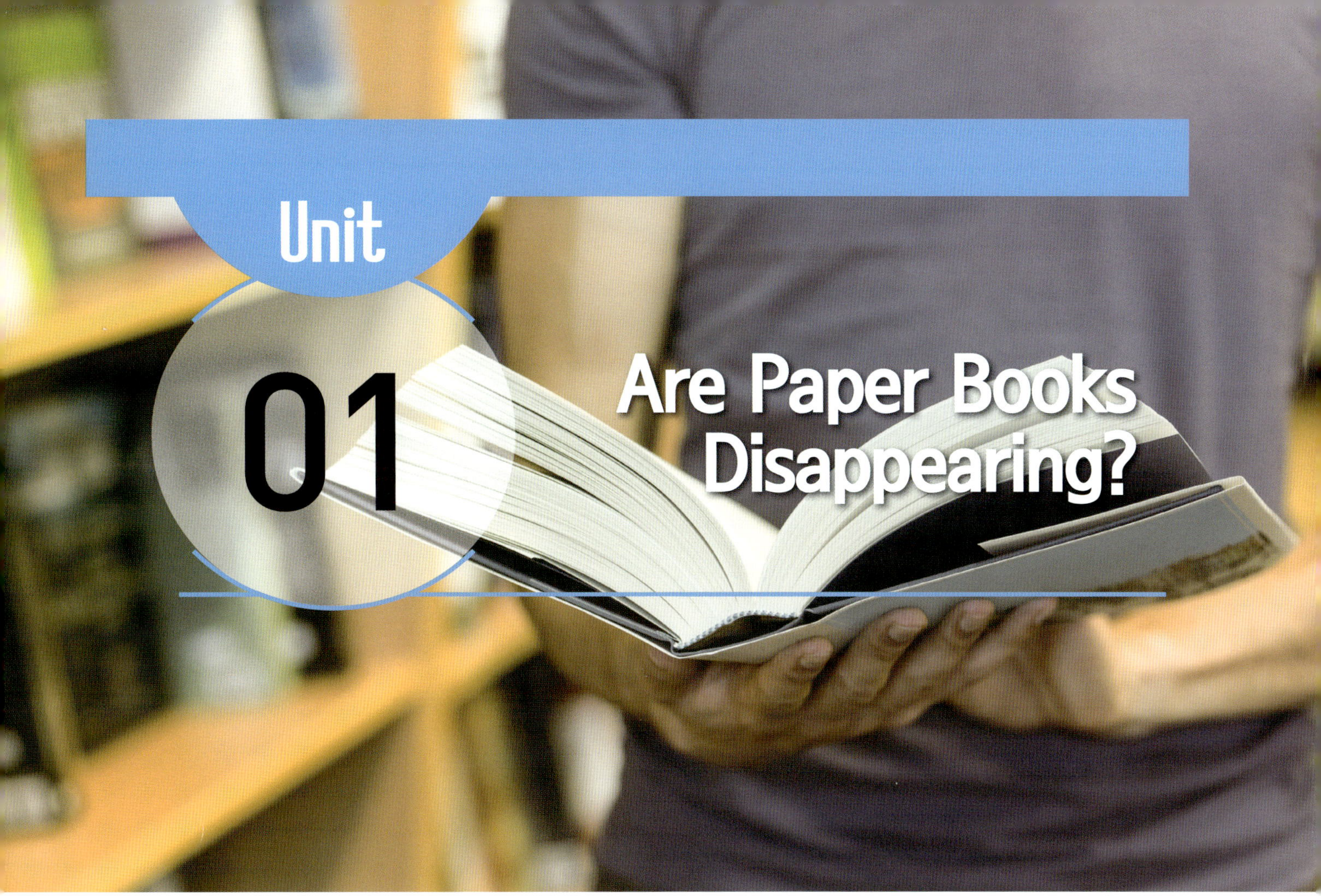

Unit 01 Are Paper Books Disappearing?

Warm Up Exercises

01 Answer these questions.

1. Do you prefer paper books or digital books?
2. Do you own any paper books?
3. Do you believe digital books to be more advantageous than paper books?

02 Put the words in right column.

Environment-friendly, Deeper Concentration, Availability, Convenient, Mental Stimulation, Relaxation, Accessible

Digital Books	Paper Books

Pre-Vocabulary Exercises

1 Match the words to their similar meaning.

1. Dyslexia	a. reading comprehension and visual difficulty
2. Traditional	b. old-fashioned
3. Contemporary	c. modern life
4. Efficient	d. not wasteful
5. Convenient	e. advantageous; user-friendly
6. Digital Age	f. an era when computers make things easier

2 Find the meaning of the following phrases.

1. Environment-friendly ______________________
2. Dominance of computer technologies

   ____
3. Lack of concentration ______________________
4. Mental Stimulation ______________________

Are Paper Books Disappearing?

How often do you read a book or a magazine article? In modern life, most people's reading habits are limited to SNS messaging, instructions given on instant soup packets, or subtitles of their favorite movies. Statistics show that the number of paper book readers has been sharply decreased in the past two decades. Paper books are considered a good friend to humans and they are the traditional form of books which has been around for centuries. Readers maintain a close relationship with a book that helps them to enjoy reading. However, with the dominance of computer technologies in this digital age, many people think digital books are more functional than paper books. They insist that the paper books are old fashioned and not convenient to carry around.

People who think digital books are better and should replace paper books argue that they are more efficient and environmental friendly. The first reason is that the digital books are always available and save time spent running to the bookstores. One digital device can store hundreds of e-books whereas several paper books may be too heavy to carry around. In addition, e-books are 50-60% cheaper than paper books. Furthermore, the availability of paper books can also become an issue sometimes when the bookstore runs out of stock. This highlights the importance of digital books since they are generally available all the time. Secondly, e-books have text-to-speech functionality that helps students with dyslexia, an abnormality that limits students' reading comprehension or visual impairment. This function reduces eye strain and may improve the learning of foreign languages.

In contrast, the proponents of paper books claim that paper books are the original and more legitimate method of reading. Firstly, studies suggest that paper books create deeper concentration than digital books. Readers of digital books face lack of concentration because of various computer functions including checking email, reading news, browsing websites, etc. In addition, reading a paper book can help one to stay mentally stimulated which may delay the onset of Alzheimer's and Dementia. It works the same way as our body muscles; the brain needs exercise to stay healthy. Secondly, reading a paper book helps to release stress and offers contentment. Research claims that six minutes of reading helps you feeling relaxed and stay calm. Furthermore, it can be a daunting task to finish an e-book unless you are very dedicated with reading. In contrast, a paper book stares at you if you do not finish it.

In conclusion, reading books is no doubt one of the best hobbies no matter how you do it. It is a personal choice that is usually based on people's circumstances in which they live. Following the benefits of both paper and e-books, it is not quite easy to negate any of them. The most important thing is to promote reading books in this age when this trend of reading books is on a sharp decline. Additionally, if people find themselves having lost everything including their job, money, and even health, their knowledge will never leave them in distress.

Main Exercises

1 Answer the questions.

Q1. Why should digital books replace paper books?

Q2. How does reading paper books improve concentration?

Q3. How do digital books help those who have reading or visual impairments?

Q4. Which medical conditions can reading books help to delay?

Q5. Other than those who have reading or visual impairments, how does the text-to-speech format help users?

2 Fill up the blanks using the words below.

impairment *traditional* *hobby* *exercise* *contentment*

1. A Hanok is an example of...................... Korean architecture.
2. He has a visual......................... in the right eye.
3. It brought a deep sense of............................ .
4. ....is good for the mind and body.
5. Her......................is to collect small souvenirs from the places she has visited.

3 Match the phrases to those given below.

1. Digital books are more accessible.
2. Paper books are inconvenient.
3. Reading paper books is good exercise for the mind.
4. Paper books can improve concentration.

a. Because there are no other distractions.

b. They can be converted into audio format.

c. It provides mental stimulation.

d. They can be heavy and difficult to acquire.

4 Summary

Fill the blanks up using the words given below and complete the summary.

mental, consume, concentration, benefits, archaic, declined, relaxed, efficient, accessible

With the era of the digital age, more people __________ information by electronics and the amount of people who read has dramatically __________ along with the number of paper books being produced. Paper books have become __________. Digital books are more __________ and better for the environment. They require no paper, take up no space, and save us money and time in acquiring them. They are __________ to those who have difficulty with reading comprehension or are visually impaired. On the other hand, paper books improve __________ because it removes any distractions. Paper books help to keep the mind sharp by providing exercise and __________ stimulation which helps delay the onset of Alzheimer's and dementia. It causes people to feel calm and __________. Whether you choose paper or digital books, reading itself is undoubtedly one of the best hobbies. They both have their strong __________ despite any disadvantages.

5 Find the mistake in each sentence and correct it by reshaping the underlined words.

1. The number of paper book readers has been sharp decreased.
2. Many people think digital books are more function than paper books.
3. Paper books are original and are the more legit method of reading.
4. Reading books helps to release stress and offer contentment.
5. Reading books is no doubt one of the best hobby no matter how you do.

6 Discussion Questions

1. Do you think that paper books will stop being produced? Why or why not?
2. Do you think that the amount of reading people do will continue to decline?
3. What are the advantages and disadvantages of digital books?
4. How can reading paper books benefit readers?
5. Do you feel that paper books are more of a harm to the environment than a benefit to readers?

7 Writing Time

Why are more people turning to digital books? Do you think paper books are beneficial or archaic? How so? Provide reasons and example to support your opinion.

Unit 02 Is Homework Helpful?

Warm Up Exercises

01 Answer these questions.

1. Which homework do you like most?
2. Which homework do you dislike most?
3. How much time do you spend doing homework every day?

02 Put the words in right column.

Independence, Boring, Better comprehension, Time management, No free time, Burden

Positive	Negative

Pre-Vocabulary Exercises

1 Match the words to their similar meaning.

1. Anxiety	**a.** analysis
2. Preparation	**b.** work
3. Prioritize	**c.** uninteresting
4. Leisure	**d.** worry
5. Labor	**e.** getting something ready
6. Review	**f.** free time
7. Boring	**g.** rank

2 Find the meaning of the following phrases.

1. Time-management ______________________________

2. Waste of time ______________________________

3. Meaningful outcome ______________________________

4. Hidden potential ______________________________

Is Homework Helpful?

Homework is a set of tasks assigned by teachers to be completed outside the classroom. Most homework includes pre-readings, writing projects, preparation for tests, or some skills to be practiced before the next class. Homework is one of the most controversial issues among many educators, parents, and students. Most students consider homework a major cause of stress that limits their outdoor activities, sleeping, and sports events. Especially in this modern era of smartphones, homework limits students' online social networking, messaging, and playing video games. Will the time ever come when there is no more homework?

People who believe in the effectiveness of homework claim that it helps them to review and understand what students learn in class. In most cases, students are very busy during class time as they learn important skills. Homework helps them to take a step back and understand what is taught in class. In addition, it helps teachers to determine how well the lessons and class contents are being understood by the students. Secondly, homework helps students to gain autonomy by thinking independently and solving problems by themselves. Students learn time management and train themselves to prioritize important tasks. Furthermore, most teachers spend a fair amount of time designing student-friendly homework that helps to reduce students' anxiety.

Critics of homework argue that homework is a waste of students' precious time. First, after a long day at school, students need some time to rest and relieve their bodies and brains from stress. Homework causes a constant disruption in enjoying family time. In addition, physical health is as important for adolescents as mental health. Students need to spend some time after school playing sports or doing other physical activities to maintain a balance between physical and mental health. Secondly, homework is considered a boring activity that seldom has any meaningful outcomes for students. Despite the efforts of teachers to design the homework for students, most pupils merely perceive it as a burden for themselves and a disruption from enjoying their free time.

In conclusion, homework carries two entirely opposite standpoints from teachers' and students' perspectives. Teachers enforce homework by believing in its hidden potential of review for students, whereas students perceive it as the enemy of their leisure and free time. Homework becomes the biggest hurdle to pursuing their modern life activities that include instant communication, multi-tasking, exciting video games, texting, and social media networking. It is important for both parents and teachers to present homework as a student-friendly task rather than making it an intense labor for students.

Main Exercises

1 Answer the questions.

Q1. How does homework help students?

Q2. How does homework help teachers?

Q3. How does homework negatively affect students life?

Q4. How does homework promote autonomy?

Q5. What are the disadvantages of homework?

2 Fill up the blanks using the words below.

controversial	*multi-tasking*	*prioritize*	*reviewed*	*independent*

1. I……………………..my family over my work.
2. He became more……………………..after he moved into his own apartment.
3. The teacher…………………...the students' homework.
4. It is difficult for her to do too many things since she is poor at ………….. .
5. This discussion in class today was very……………………………. .

3 Match the phrases to those given below.

1. Students don't spend much time with their family or friends.
2. The teacher reviewed the students' homework.
3. Student have a lot of stress.
4. Homework promotes autonomy.

a. They are often too busy with homework.

b. There is too much difficult homework.

c. So students become independent.

d. To make sure the students understood the lesson.

4 Summary

Fill up the blanks using the words below and complete the summary.

stress, independence, meaningful, polarizing, difficult, support, overwhelming, age, understand

Homework is a ___________ topic among educators, parents, and students. Those who ___________ homework believe that it helps students to better ___________ what is being taught in class as well as to gain ___________ and life skills. On the other side, those who are against it claim that it gains no ___________ results but rather it is only a major source of ___________ and limits students' time to do anything they enjoy. In this modern ___________ of social media networking, texting, and video games, it is ___________ for students to do homework. It is necessary that teachers and parents find ways to present homework that is not so ___________ and strenuous for students.

5 Find the mistake in each sentence and correct it by reshaping the underlined words.

1. Teachers spend a fair amount of time design student-friendly homework.
2. Students can think independent and solve problems by themselves.
3. Students need to spend some time play sports.
4. Homework help students to review and understand what they learn in class.
5. Students train themselves to priority important tasks.

6 Discussion Questions

1. Does homework affect a person's time to do things they enjoy?
2. Does homework have meaningful results?
3. Do teachers do enough to make homework student-friendly? Or it is often too difficult?
4. Why is homework losing its importance these days?
5. Are the benefits of doing homework really worth it compared to its disadvantages?

7 Writing Time

Do you believe that homework should continue to be given out to students? Provide reasons and examples to support your opinion.

Unit 03 Should English be a National Language of Korea?

Warm Up Exercises

01 Answer these questions.

1. What is the most commonly spoken language around the world?
2. Name at least 3 European languages.
3. How many languages can you speak?

02 Put the words in right column.

Steak, Kimchi, Samgyupsal, Apple, Hanbok, Soccer, Flower

English Words	Korean Words

Pre-Vocabulary Exercises

1 Match the words to their similar meaning.

1. Institution	**a.** conventional
2. Mainstream	**b.** not public
3. Private	**c.** formation
4. Structure	**d.** approximate
5. Creativity	**e.** academy
6. Estimate	**f.** lighten
7. Communicate	**g.** originality
8. Alleviate	**h.** interact

2 Find the meaning of the following phrases.

1. National language ______________________________

2. Educational institution ______________________________

3. At the moment ______________________________

4. Growing trend ______________________________

Should English be a National Language of Korea?

English is the most commonly spoken language across the world. According to one estimate, 28% of world population learns, uses, or at least understands English at the moment. English is the official language of 53 countries. That means, there are a lot of people in the world who are able to communicate in English. Korea is one of the most advanced countries in the world where English is considered an important skill to master. Koreans spend a sizable amount of their income on the English education of their children and adults. Considering Korean's interest in and effort for learning English, some people suggest that English should be declared a national language of South Korea, whereas other disagree claiming that this might hurt the development of the Korean language.

People, who think English should become a national language of Korea, present two reasons. First, declaring English as a national language of Korea will help schools adopt English as a mainstream language without any prejudice. These days, Korean is used as the medium of instruction in educational institutions. Once English is declared a national language of Korea, schools will base their curriculum on the needs of modern world. This could solve one of the biggest problems in Korean education system. Second, declaring English as a national language of Korea will help alleviate Korean parents' financial burden surrounding their children's English education. Most Korean parents spend a lot of money on their children's private education and English is the main part of these expenses. Having English as a mainstream language at the school level will mitigate their private English education spending.

The opponents of English to be a national language think that this will affect all

the efforts to promote Korean language and culture internationally. First, they believe that if English becomes one of Korea's national languages, then the Korean language itself will be in danger. The growing trend of learning English is already influencing the promotion of Korean language. Thus, this could change the whole cultural and historical dynamic of Korea if English becomes Korea's national language. Second, Korea has achieved the status of the world's 10th biggest economy without English as its national language. This means, Koreans have made all this progress using the Korean language. Changing the basis of language structure in Korea may hurt Korea's progress towards its productivity and creativity.

In conclusion, both sides have their merits and demerits. The important thing to consider is making economic progress and maintaining national identity at the same time. Promoting the English language in Korea is a great path towards globalization. However, at the same time, it is important to preserve the Korean identity and its culture.

Main Exercises

1 Answer the questions.

Q1. How many countries in the world use English as the official language?

Q2. How much of the world's population learns, uses, or understands English?

Q3. In which way will using English as a national language help Koreans financially?

Q4. How big is the economy of Korea?

Q5. How will changing the basic language structure in Korea hurt its progress?

2 Fill up the blanks using the words below.

private	*institution*	*creativity*	*communicate*	*alleviate*

1. She hired a .... detective to solve the mystery.
2. .... is the most important element in writing.
3. For a good teamwork, you need to .... with your teammates.
4. The doctor used painkillers to.............................. his patient's agony.
5. He used to work in a(n) .... as a teacher for fifteen years.

3 Match the phrases to those given below.

1. I'm busy cooking hamburgers at the moment.
2. The national language of Australia
3. Rap music is a growing trend among young people.
4. She was sent to a private educational institution.

a. So I'll call you later.

b. Because her parents thought ordinary schools were not good enough for her.

c. Because of its rebellious messages and its rhythmic beats.

d. Is English.

4 Summary

Fill the blanks up using the words given below and complete the summary.

national language, education, curriculum, dynamic, population, financial, progress, change

English is the most commonly spoken language in the world. It is learnt, used and understood by about 28% of the world ________ and is the official language in 53 countries. Declaring English as the national language of Korea will help schools base their ________ the same way as the needs of the modern world. Not only that, it will ease the ________ burden of paying for private _______ for Korean parents as well. However, some worry that changing the ___________ will danger the Korean language itself by influencing the cultural and historic ________ of Korea, and claim that Korea has achieved a large economy without English as a national language, and therefore will not need to _______ the main language. Though opinions may differ, the most important thing is to make economic ________ while keeping national identity simultaneously.

5 Find the mistake in each sentence and correct the underlined words.

1. People cannot live without communicate with others.
2. It is estimates that about 28% of the world understands English.
3. The growing trend of learning English is affect the promotion of Korean language.
4. Many public and private institutions teaching English to students.
5. Koreans have make all the social and economic progress using Korean language.

6 Discussion Questions

1. Do you think English may replace Korean as the national language? Why or why not?
2. How can we reduce education costs?
3. Is English an easy language to learn compared to other languages? Why or why not?
4. Which foreign language would you like to learn the most? why?
5. What are the benefits of knowing more than one language?

7 Writing Time

Is it a good idea to choose a certain language as the global language; the only language in the world? Will it make it possible to communicate freely with everyone in the world or will it wipe out cultural differences? What are the pros and cons of a universal language? State reasons and provide examples to support your opinion.

Unit 04 Is Studying Abroad Beneficial?

Warm Up Exercises

01 **Answer these questions.**

1. Have you ever studied abroad?
2. Name at least 3 subjects you study.
3. Name at least seven countries.

02 **Put the words in right column.**

Seoul, United states, Paris, London, Egypt, Italy

Country	City

Pre-Vocabulary Exercises

1 Match the words to their similar meaning.

1. Instinctually	a. blockades
2. homesickness	b. rising rapidly
3. frustration	c. tutoring
4. anxiety	d. anguish
5. tuition	e. nervousness
6. soaring	f. a sickness happening from being away from home
7. barriers	g. acting on instinct

2 Find the meaning of the following phrases.

1. Self-confidence ______________________
2. New language ______________________
3. Part time jobs ______________________
4. Culture shock ______________________

Is Studying Abroad Beneficial?

Learning is something that impacts nearly every aspect of human existence every day. Instinctually, human beings are constantly learning new things, or expounding on existing knowledge. Some people pursue their desire of learning in foreign nations and take in the glamor and culture of new lands. Studying abroad means going to a foreign country for a certain duration of time to study. Studying in another country may be one of the most beneficial and, at the same time, most challenging experiences a student can have in life. This gives students the opportunity to see the world and learn about a unique culture. However, some people disagree that studying abroad helps students' learning.

The main reason people choose to study abroad is that it opens new doors for students to shape their future. Firstly, it equips students with independence, self-confidence, and maturity. By studying abroad, people experience a new country with incredible new outlooks, customs, and activities. The benefits of studying abroad include the prospect of seeing new terrain, natural wonders, museums, and landmarks in the foreign nation. In addition, learning a new language and making new friends are the popular draws for people who want to study abroad. Secondly, studying abroad grants the possibility to completely immerse oneself in a new language; and there is no better way to learn a new language than to live among the native speakers of that language. This helps to get closer to local people and make many new friends.

People who disagree the idea of studying abroad argue that it is a big burden on the students and their families if they choose to live in another country for education purposes. Firstly, students have to pay high tuition fees and bear soaring living expenses which vary greatly depending on the country and educational institution. This may cause an extra burden to not only the students, but also to their parents. The burden to pay off bills forces many students to take on long-hour part-time jobs to meet the expenses. Secondly, students who live in other countries for studies face language barriers. When living in a foreign country, it is important to possess a certain level of fluency that is expected from the peers and the locals with whom the students need to be communicating abroad. Furthermore, culture shock may jolt students studying in a new country. These culture shocks often stem from poor language ability. In most cases, the culture shocks lead to feelings of frustration, anxiety, and homesickness among students.

In conclusion, studying abroad seems like an excellent chance for students to learn a different culture and a new language. This can open new doors for students to shape their future plans. Studying abroad teaches students independence, self-confidence, and maturity. Whereas, it may cast negative impression on students because of heavy cost, language barriers, and culture shocks. The best way to face these challenges is to prepare in advance, getting enough knowledge of the host country's culture, and learning basic communication language before going to study abroad.

Main Exercises

1 Answer the questions.

Q1. What is important when living in a foreign country?

Q2. What are reasons why people study abroad?

Q3. What kind of negative effects can culture shock have on students?

Q4. Is studying in a foreign country expensive?

Q5. What is the best way to face challenges while studying abroad?

2 Fill up the blanks using the words below.

barriers *anxiety* *culture shock* *homesickness* *tuition*

1. Staying abroad for too long can cause ....
2. Feeling of .... can appear when going to a foreign country for the first time.
3. Eating dog meat was a .... to many foreigners.
4. Language .... can make life overseas complicated.
5. Private .... fees can become very expensive.

3 Match the phrases to those given below.

1. Learning a new language
2. Culture shock appears
3. Part time jobs are the best way for students to make money.
4. It is important to have self confidence.

a. When faced with a new culture.

b. Because they are easy and temporary

c. Can be a challenging decision.

d. Before making a presentation.

4 Summary

Fill the blanks up using the words given below and complete the summary.

tuition, immerse, homesickness, self-confidence, beneficial, culture shock, barriers

Learning is something that impacts nearly every aspect of human existence every day. Studying abroad can be one of the most _____________ yet challenging events in life. The main reason why people study abroad is because it opens new doors for students to shape their future. It equips students with independence, ____________ and maturity. Also, it can make new friends and one can completely __________ oneself into learning a new language. However, learning abroad has expensive ________ and living costs, which can cause extra burden to students and parents. Plus, students face language ___________ overseas as well as ___________, which can lead to feelings of frustration, anxiety and __________. Studying abroad can be an excellent experience, but getting enough of the host country's culture and language is also important.

5 Find the mistake in each sentence and correct the underlined words.

1. Culture shock can lead to some <u>metal</u> symptoms.
2. The financial burden <u>casting</u> on students studying abroad is quite immense.
3. Learning a new language and making new friends are the popular draws for people who want to <u>studying</u> abroad.
4. Learning is something that <u>to impact</u> nearly every aspect of human existence everyday.

6 Discussion Questions

Q1. How can we reduce the costs of studying abroad?

Q2. How can we deal with troubling emotions which come from studying abroad?

Q3. What are the benefits of studying in one's homeland?

Q4. What are some ways to overcome homesickness?

7 Writing Time

Is homestay a good idea when people study abroad? Does it serve as a cheap way to study abroad or can it lead to other problems? What are the pros and cons of homestay? Provide reasons and examples to support your opinion.

Unit 05 Are Sports better than Gym Exercises?

Warm Up Exercises

01 **Answer these questions.**

1. What does the term 'exercise' mean?
2. Have you ever tried working out?
3. Name at least three exercise methods.

02 **Put the words in right column.**

Hockey, Traveling, Cricket, Baseball, Dining out, Taking pictures, Drawing, Squash

Sports	Non-sports

Pre-Vocabulary Exercises

1 Match the words to their similar meaning.

1. Distract	**a.** supportable
2. Dedication	**b.** player
3. Sustainable	**c.** involve
4. Athlete	**d.** devotion
5. Engage	**e.** divert
6. Adolescents	**f.** teenagers
7. Ultimate	**g.** final

2 Find the meaning of the following phrases.

1. Physical health ______________________

2. Self-esteem ______________________

3. Strong connection ______________________

4. well-structured ______________________

Are Sports better than Gym Exercises?

Exercising is a natural way to release stress and stay in shape. Exercising offers a great platform to make new friends and socialize. Both gym exercise and playing a sport require lots of time, strength, and dedication. Some people think that playing a sport distracts students from their studying and it is a waste of time. They propose that gym exercise is more helpful for people with busy schedules. However, studies suggest that organized and well-structured youth sports can provide many benefits for people of all ages. Team sports teach adolescents responsibility, commitment, and leadership skills. Therefore, many people consider team sports more beneficial than exercising in the gym.

People who think gym exercise provides more benefits to humans claim that gym exercise boosts memory and the ability to learn new things. Firstly, getting sweaty while working out in the gym enhances production of memory cells in the brain that helps to learn faster. Therefore, some researchers relate children's brain health with their physical fitness. A study showed that weight training at the gym or running on treadmills helps with vocabulary retention. A 30 minutes' workout helps to alleviate anxiety for most people who get stressed after long working hours. In addition, gym exercise has a strong connection with sleeping habits. Secondly, gym exercise is a sustainable activity that does not depend on weather, time, or other people. Most gyms are open from morning till night that offer people a chance to work out in their free time. Most outdoor sports are weather dependent. If the weather is not ideal, people cannot exercise.

On the other hand, some critics of gym exercise argue that team sports have more benefits. Firstly, team sports offer leadership skills to athletes. Fighting for a common goal with other athletes and coaches helps to build teamwork and to effectively communicate to solve problems. The experience an athlete obtains during a sport can be helpful when experiencing problems in daily life. Therefore, participating in a team sport can develop a strong character. This also boosts self-esteem that results in reducing pressure and anxiety. Secondly, team sports are important for physical health because they provide more strength to the body than simple gym exercises. One of the reasons is that at the gym many people feel bored and consider exercising a burden, whereas team sports are an interactive activity that engages all participants. These athletes forget their worries and show a lot of interest and passion. Some researchers also connect it to human brain development; when people play with other team members, their brains release happy endorphins.

In conclusion, both the team sports and the gym exercises have their own benefits. The most important thing is dedication and commitment to exercise to maintain our health. Based on individual choices and interests, choosing how to engage our body in physical activity is important. Some bodies are more suitable for active field sports whereas the others tend to develop more strength through gym exercise. The ultimate goal of exercise is to stay healthy and be happy in life.

Main Exercises

1 Answer the questions.

Q1. How do gym exercises boost memory?

Q2. What helps students with vocabulary retention?

Q3. How much exercise reduces stress for most people?

Q4. What skills do team sports offer?

Q5. How do some people feel at the gym?

2 Fill up the blanks using the words below.

release *ultimate* *teamwork* *gym* *exercise*

1. Gym ________________ provides many benefits to humans.
2. Weight training at the _____________ helps for remembering vocabulary.
3. Fighting for a common goal with others helps to build __________________ .
4. Spending time with family helps brains to ________________ happy endorphins.
5. The ____________________ goal of earning money is to enjoy a happy in life.

3 Match the phrases to those given below.

1. Participating in a team sport can,
2. If the weather is not ideal,
3. The ultimate goal of exercise is
4. Exercising is a natural way.

a. People cannot exercise.

b. To stay healthy and happy in life.

c. Develop a strong character.

d. To release stress and stay in shape.

4 Summary

Fill the blanks up using the words given below and complete the summary.

people, leadership, stress, dedication, advocate, schedules, engage

Exercising is a natural way to release ______________ and stay in shape. Both the gym exercises and playing a sport need lots of time, strength, and ______________. Some people think that playing a sport distracts students from their study and it is a waste of time. They ______________ that gym exercise is more helpful for people with busy ______________. However, studies suggest that organized and well-structured youth sports can provide many benefits for people of all ages. Team sports teach ______________ responsibility, commitment, and ___________ skills. Based on individual choices and interests, choosing how to ______________ our body in physical activity is important.

5 Find the mistake in each sentence and correct the underlined words.

1. It is important to engaging our body in physical activity.
2. Team sport develop a strong character.
3. Most gyms offers people a chance to work out at night.
4. Exercise help reducing anxiety and stress.
5. Working out provides strengthen to our brains.

6 Discussion Questions

Q1. What are the benefits of gym exercises?

Q2. What are the benefits of team sports?

Q3. Which sports are weather dependent?

Q4. Why some people think gym exercises are boring?

Q5. How do team sports develop leadership skills?

7 Writing Time

Why some people prefer team sports to gym exercise? Provide reasons and examples to support your opinion.

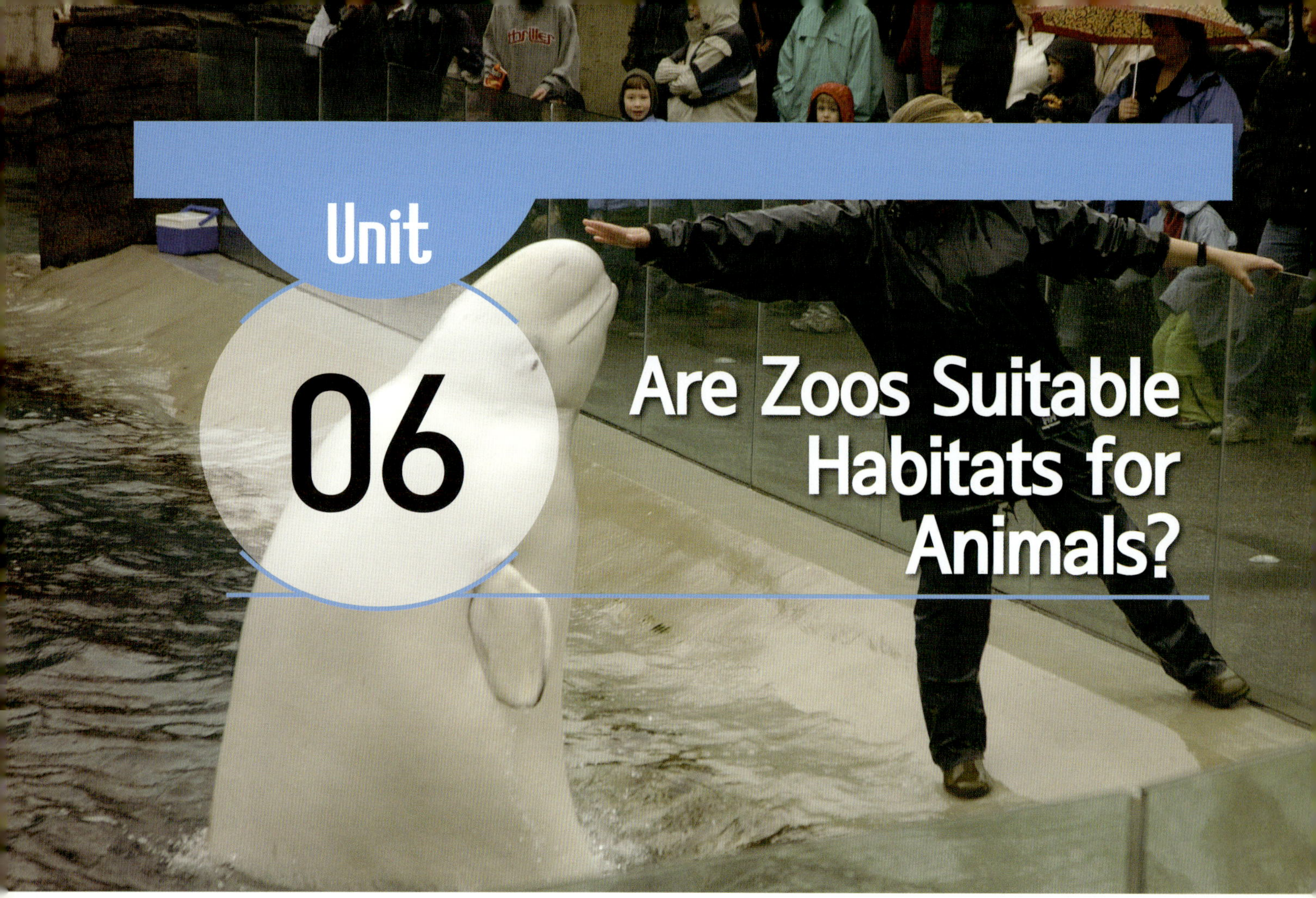

Unit 06 Are Zoos Suitable Habitats for Animals?

Warm Up Exercises

01 **Answer these questions.**

1. What does it mean by 'habitat'?
2. How often do you visit zoos?
3. When was the first time you visited a zoo?

02 **Put the words in right column.**

Natural, Captivity, Dangerous, Zookeepers, Visitors, Hunters

Zoo	Wild

Pre-Vocabulary Exercises

1 Match the words to their similar meaning.

1. Breed	a. doctors for animal
2. Abuse	b. ethics
3. Lifesaving	c. next to
4. Veterinarian	d. give birth
5. Haven	e. rescue
6. Morality	f. misuse
7. Alongside	g. shelter

2 Find the meaning of the following phrases.

1. Endangered animals ______________________
2. In-depth ______________________
3. Conservation center ______________________
4. Local people ______________________

Are Zoos Suitable Habitats for Animals?

Zoos have been a part of human history since the very beginning. Zoos are great places that offer visitors the chance to view lots of different animals confined in a safe area. Many zoos have breeding programs that help to breed endangered animals. They also offer local people an opportunity to learn about animals and nature. This helps to engage children in science and to discover about nature. Besides various benefits, some activists think that zoos are places where animals are generally abused. Do zoos really help to conserve animals?

Proponents of zoos insist that zoos are great conservation facilities for endangered animals. Firstly, zoos can provide caring and lifesaving treatment to endangered animals to conserve them. Veterinarians are available at most zoos who can take good care of sick animals. In other words, zoos are a safe haven for animals who might be in danger. Furthermore, zoos are also an important economic resource for the community. Lots of businesses are associated with zoos that help to bring prosperity in the community. Secondly, zoos provide a great educational resource for both children and adults. Zookeepers are trained with specific knowledge about the animals. They provide necessary information about animals' behavior, habitat, and instincts to the visitors. In addition, zoos provide university students a facility to perform in-depth research on specific animals for their degree programs. This research not only helps students to complete their degree programs, but it also helps the government to make new policies regarding animals' care and protection.

Some activists argue that keeping animals in zoos for any reason is unethical. Firstly, holding any animal in a zoo raises many questions on human morality. Most animals are born with the instincts of living in the wild. Keeping them in captivity means we believe they are inferior to humans. Furthermore, captivity also affects their chances of survival. For example, killer whales live up to 100 years in wild; however, they can only survive in zoos for maximum 30 years. Secondly, animals are treated badly by visitor at zoos. Some visitors throw objects at animals which has a negative effect on animals. This results in serious physical and mental harm to the animals. In addition, zoos can set a bad example for children. They may think that it is okay to keep animals in captivity.

To sum up, the debate of whether zoos are good or bad places is never ending. It is undeniable that zoos contribute to learning about animals' behavior, and define measures to protect them. However, some visitors and zookeepers' bad behavior violates animals' right. It is very important to recognize the equal rights of animals to exist on this planet alongside humans. Zoos should strictly be used as conservation centers; and if they are to become a public attraction, then the visitors have to be trained to be polite and respectful toward animals.

Main Exercises

1 Answer the questions.

Q1. What can zoos provide to the university students?

Q2. What does keeping animals in captivity mean?

Q3. How long do killer whales live in captivity?

Q4. How do zoos help endangered animal?

Q5. What do zookeepers provide to the visitors?

2 Fill up the blanks using the words below.

lifesaving *abuse* *haven* *veterinarian* *breed*

1. Most sharks ……………………6 to 12 babies at a time.
2. Child ……………………is one of the serious problems.
3. Hospitals are for a ……………………operation.
4. The dog needs a ……………………to be cured.
5. My house is the best ……………………for me.

3 Match the phrases to those given below.

1. Zoos are an important economic resource for the community.
2. Zoos provide university students a facility to perform in-depth research.
3. Zoos can set a wrong example for children.
4. Veterinarians are available at most zoos.

a. Lots of businesses are associated with zoos.

b. They may think that it is okay to keep animals in captivity.

c. They can take good care of sick animals.

d. It helps the government to make new policies regarding animals' care.

4 Summary

Fill the blanks up using the words given below and complete the summary.

resource, treatment, abused, physically, strictly, superior

Zoos have been a part of human history since the very beginning. However, some people think that zoos are the places where animals are generally ____________ . Proponents of zoos insist that zoos can provide a caring and lifesaving ____________ to endangered animals to conserve them. Secondly, zoos provide a great educational ____________ for both children and adults. On the other hand, some activists argue that holding any animal in a zoo raises many questions on human morality such as believing that humans are ____________ to them. Moreover, animals are treated badly by visitor at zoos which can mentally and ____________ harm them. In conclusion, Zoos should ____________ be used as conservation centers and the visitors have to be trained to be polite and respectful toward animals.

5 Find the mistake in each sentence and correct it by reshaping the underlined words.

1. Zoos have been a part of human history since the much beginning.
2. Do the zoos really help to conserved animals?
3. Lots of businesses are associated in zoos.
4. Killer whales live to 100 years in wild.
5. It helps the government to make new policies regarded animals' care and protection.

6 Discussion Questions

1. What is the difference between wild animals and domesticated animals?
2. Do animals in zoos want to be free? Why or why not?
3. What do wild animals need from human?
4. Are zoos essential for humans and animals?
5. What are the problems associated with zoos?

7 Writing Time

Are zoos important for humans and animals? What are pros and cons of zoos? Provide reasons and examples to support your opinion.

Unit 07 Are Co-education Systems Effective?

Warm Up Exercises

01 Answer these questions.

1. What does it mean by co-education?
2. Think about advantages of single-sex education.
3. Think about advantages of co-education.

02 Put the words in right column.

Changes, Job, Marriage, High school, Parent, Growth

Adult	Adolescent

Pre-Vocabulary Exercises

1 Match the words to their similar meaning.

1. Grade	a. provide
2. Separate	b. have an effect on
3. Influence	c. cleanliness
4. Hygiene	d. exclusively
5. Limit	e. disconnected
6. Solely	f. rank
7. Offer	g. restrict

2 Find the meaning of the following phrases.

1. Interact with ________________________________
2. Care about ________________________________
3. Sexual harassment ________________________________
4. Mental development ________________________________

Are Co-education Systems Effective?

According to the newspaper Korea Herald, 85% of coeducation school students get higher grades on the Korean Scholastic Aptitude Test compared to gender separate schools' students. Older thinking states that "coeducation has a bad influence on students," however, this seems not to be true anymore. Many believe that boys and girls should be in a co-education system because it helps them to learn how to interact with the opposite gender, helps to improve their hygiene by encouraging better appearance, and enables them to improve social skills. On the other hand, the opponents consider co-education systems a big distraction for young learners that limits their creativity.

Opponents of coeducation claim that coeducation is a main cause of disruption in students' learning. Firstly, students in coeducation care more about their appearance and less about their learning. The teenage years are an important part of students' lives that shape their future careers. It requires them to focus solely on their studies, creativity, and skill development rather than struggling with gender interaction related issues. Ultimately, they get many chances to have interactions with other genders once they are in college or at their workplaces. Secondly, teenagers go through a phase of puberty that increases their curiosity toward other genders. In coeducation, this sometimes triggers unwanted incidents like sexual harassment. In addition, students in coeducation remain under constant mental stress as they may feel like they are always watched and judged by many other students which might affect their personality development.

On the other hand, proponents of coeducation consider it beneficial for students' mental development. Firstly, co-education helps to educate students how to respond to their curiosity toward the opposite gender. Studying with opposite gender students in the same classroom all day provides lots of opportunities to learn about each other. Studies claim that students show better performance in a coeducation setting than those in separate education. Secondly, coeducation improves students' sense of hygiene by encouraging more focus on appearance in the presence of other gender students. In addition, cleanliness maintains health which improves concentration for study. It can easily be seen in co-education schools that students regularly brush their teeth after meals, get proper haircuts, and wear clean clothes. Furthermore, co-education helps to improve interpersonal skills that brings lots of excitement in life.

In conclusion, it seems coeducation offers lots of benefits to students including learning about other genders, improving hygiene, and developing social skills. However, some consider coeducation a distraction for students' learning. It is important that learners should have a chance to choose their favorite system. Some feel more comfortable in coeducation while others show better performance in a separate education system. It is the parents' duty to determine their children's interests before deciding their schools.

Main Exercises

1 Answer the questions.

Q1. What percentage of co-educational students gets higher grades on the test?

Q2. Why could sexual harassment happen in co-education schools?

Q3. Why do students in co-education suffer from mental stress?

Q4. How can co-education help students improve their senses of hygiene?

Q5. Why is improving interpersonal skills important?

2 Fill up the blanks using the words below.

separately *grade* *limit* *solely* *influence*

1. I got a low .... in the math test.
2. The brothers live .... in different countries.
3. My boss's speech gave me a positive .... on my work.
4. Never .... yourself or you will come to a standstill.
5. Do not rely .... on your parents after you are all grown up.

3 Match the phrases to those given below.

1. Co-education improves students' hygiene.
2. Students must focus solely on their studies.
3. Co-education is beneficial for mental development.
4. Students remain in stress in Co-education schools.

a. Because students learn from other gender.

b. Because they are always judged and watched by other students.

c. Teenage years are for shaping their future career.

d. They regularly brush their teeth, get proper haircut, and wear clean clothes.

4 Summary

Fill the blanks up using the words given below and complete the summary.

sexual, system, beneficial, interpersonal, focus, care, recent

Older thinking used to ___________________ on a bad influence of co-education. However, _______________ studies revealed that co-education has a lot of advantages. Opponents of co-education say It will force students to _______________ about their appearance. It could also cause _______________ harassment and mental stress. Proponents of co-education believe it is _______________ for satisfying their curiosity. Furthermore, it will boost students' senses of hygiene and improve _______________ skills. Therefore, it is vital to make sure that students choose their favorite _______________.

5 Find the mistake in each sentence and correct it by reshaping the underlined words.

1. This seems not be true anymore.
2. Students in coeducation remaining under constant mental stress.
3. It might effect their personality development.
4. Studying together provide lots of opportunities.
5. Co-education improves sense of hygiene by encourage more focus on appearance

6 Discussion Questions

1. Which school system do you prefer?
2. Is caring about appearance really helpful for students?
3. Why do students in co-education schools feel like they are being watched?
4. Are students in single-sex school lack social skills?
5. What are other benefits of co-education?

7 Writing Time

If you were a parent of a child, which school would you prefer for your child? And why? Provide reasons and examples to support your opinion.

Unit 08

Should Plastic Bags Be Banned?

Warm Up Exercises

01 **Answer these questions.**

1. When do you usually use plastic bags?
2. How many plastic bags do you have in your home?
3. Which do you prefer paper bags or plastic bags?

02 **Put the words in right column.**

Stubborn, Eco-friendly, Delicate, Cheaper, Water-proof, Made of wood

Paper bag	Plastic bag

Pre-Vocabulary Exercises

1 Match the words to their similar meaning.

1. Grocery	**a.** drift
2. Sustainable	**b.** mess up
3. Manner	**c.** continuous
4. Pollute	**d.** means
5. Litter	**e.** contaminate
6. Float	**f.** polluted
7. Contaminated	**g.** food

2 Find the meaning of the following phrases.

1. Standing debate ____________________

2. Potential threat ____________________

3. In turn ____________________

4. Cost effective ____________________

Should Plastic Bags Be Banned?

Plastic bags are a convenient way to carry things when shopping. They have been a part of our life for past few decades. There are numerous advantages to plastic grocery bags, and by recycling them diligently, consumers can profit from their use in a more environmentally sustainable manner. However, many experts consider them a potential threat to the environment. Environmental scientists regard plastic bags as a serious problem for human health and global warming. There has been a long standing debate about whether to use plastic bags or paper bags for shopping.

Opponents of the use of plastic bags argue that plastic bags pollute our land and water. Since the plastic bags are so light, they can travel long distances by wind or water. They litter the land by getting caught in fences and trees, floating in water, and blocking the water drains. Secondly, plastic bags are harmful to animals and fish. Animals, birds, and fish often mistakenly consume them as food which in turn causes digestive problems and can even lead to death. Furthermore, humans eat the contaminated fish which can cause serious health problems for people. In addition, animals and fish are often entangled in this plastic which can cause serious injuries.

On the other hand, proponents of using plastic bags argue that plastic bags are one of the most important parts of our daily life. Firstly, plastic bags are cost effective, easy to use, and more durable. Stores buy plastic bags in bulk at a nominal price that reduces the overall goods price for customer. In addition, plastic bags are quicker to open, pack stuff, and double up than paper bags, whereas, paper bags are at least two times more expensive than plastic bags. Secondly, plastic bags are more durable than paper bags. They are less likely to tear, easier to carry, and more useful in rain. They can easily become a trash can liner, or can be used to pack various items. Comparatively, plastic bags last longer and can be washed out to be reused, whereas, paper bags are generally less durable, difficult to carry, and cannot be reused.

In conclusion, experts still have lots of concerns about the use of plastic bags due to their bad effects on the environment and human health. In addition, plastic bags pose threats to other creatures including animals, birds, and fish. The counter opinion suggests that plastic bags are one of the modern life's most important needs. Plastic bags make shopping convenient and are reusable. It is important for both the government and the public to cooperate in order to find solutions to reduce the negative effects of plastic bags. An awareness campaign of the effective use of plastic bags needs to be launched. In order to get the most benefits of the available resources, we must reuse plastic bags as much as possible before recycling them.

Main Exercises

1 Answer the questions.

Q1. Why are plastic bags easy to use?

Q2. How can plastic bags cause digestive problems in animals?

Q3. How can plastic bags harm human's health?

Q4. How can plastic bags cause injuries to animals?

Q5. What are shortcomings of paper bags?

2 Fill up the blanks using the words below.

manner *float* *grocery* *sustainable* *contaminated*

1. I bought some snacks at a ……………….…. store.
2. Korea needs a new ………..…………….. energy.
3. You need to try it in a different…………………….. .
4. Clouds………………….. in the sky.
5. The river has been……………… by toxic waste.

3 Match the phrases to those given below.

1. Experts consider plastic bags a potential threat to the environment.
2. Plastic bags can cause serious health problems for people.
3. Plastic bags can travel long distance by wind and water.
4. Plastic bags are cost effective.

a. Stores buy plastic bags in bulk at a nominal price.
b. They are so light.
c. When humans eat the contaminated fish which consumed plastic bags.
d. They think plastic bags can trigger human health problems and global warming.

4 Summary

Fill the blanks up using the words given below and complete the summary.

mistakenly, effective, potential, durable, past, light

Plastic bags have been a part of our life for ______________ few decades. There are numerous advantages of plastic bags but many experts consider them a ______________ threat to the environment. Opponents say they pollute the land by traveling a long distance since they are so ______________. Moreover, they can cause serious health problems to animals and humans by ______________ consuming them. However, proponents insist that plastic bags are necessary for our life. They are cost effective, easy to use, and more ______________. In conclusion, the government and the public need to plan an awareness campaign of the ______________ use of plastic bags.

GREEN PAPER PRODUCTS™

5 Find the mistake in each sentence and correct it by reshaping the underlined words.

1. Animals often <u>mistaken</u> consume plastic bags.
2. Humans eat the <u>contaminating</u> fish.
3. Animals are often <u>entangle</u> in plastic bags.
4. <u>Animal</u> are often entangled in plastic bags.
5. An awareness campaign needs to be <u>launch</u>.

6 Discussion Questions

1. Think of at least 5 ways for the effective use of plastic bags.
2. Do you think people should stop using plastic bags? Why or why not?
3. Are paper bags harmful to nature? How?
4. Why are plastic bags cheaper than paper bags?
5. Is there any other option besides paper bags and plastic bags?

7 Writing Time

Should people stop using plastic bags? Is there any way to use plastic bags without harming the environment? Provide reasons and examples to support your opinion.

Unit 09 Are Interracial Marriages Successful?

Warm Up Exercises

01 **Answer these questions.**

1. What does it mean by 'interracial marriage'?
2. Do you know anyone who is in an interracial marriage?
3. Is interracial marriage viewed positively in Korea?

02 **Put the words in right column.**

Children, Alone, Wedding, Honeymoon, Individual, Freedom

Marriage	Single

Pre-Vocabulary Exercises

1 Match the words to their similar meaning.

1. Globalization	a. disadvantage
2. Charm	b. create
3. Drawback	c. engage
4. Involve	d. worldwide integration
5. Form	e. attraction
6. Interracial	f. dishonor
7. Stigma	g. intercultural

2 Find the meaning of the following phrases.

1. Considerable rise ______________________
2. Interracial marriage ______________________
3. Developing country ______________________
4. Developed country ______________________

Are Interracial Marriages Successful?

Interracial marriage is a marriage outside a social group, community, or tribe. Interracial marriage can also be referred to as mixed or intercultural marriage. One of the effects of globalization is a considerable rise in interracial marriages in developing and developed countries. People in interracial marriages do not give importance to skin color, tribe, religion, or physical difference as long as a strong relationship exists between them. Besides lots of excitement and charm, there are some challenges and drawbacks for those involved in interracial marriages. Therefore, people in each society have varied opinions about interracial marriages.

The proponents of interracial marriages argue that interracial marriages are more successful and interesting. Firstly, people involved in interracial marriage have a very high level of acceptance towards their spouse's culture, values, and beliefs. This develops a better understanding, cooperation, and respect for each other that forms the basis of a successful marriage. Secondly, interracial couples never run out of topics to talk about. They share wonderful and diverse ideas, childhood stories, and their languages and history. In addition, interracial marriages often create unique and beautiful children. These children may inherit the best features of both parents. Furthermore, marrying someone from a different race helps to break negative stereotypes about that race.

On the flip side, opponents of interracial marriages argue that they are full of challenges and hardships for both individuals involved. Firstly, in most cases, biracial children face high levels of discrimination, stigma, and lack of acceptance from society. Some conservative people may criticize, taunt, and bully them emotionally and even harm them physically. Secondly, parenting styles could be a major cause of disagreement between the couples. Interracial couples may have different ways to bring up their children due to the different environments in which they grew up. In addition, families of interracial couples may have trouble interacting with each other due to language barriers.

To sum up, interracial marriages is a growing trend that contains both merits and demerits. Besides some concerns, most people have positive opinions about interracial marriages. They offer couples an opportunity to learn the uniqueness of each other's culture, understand each other ethics, moral standards, and ways of life. They will also be able to learn each other's language, food, religion, music, fashion, and arts. In order to avoid clashes and enjoy successful marriage life, it is important for interracial couples to compromise in the areas that they disagree about and come together in the areas that they agree on.

Main Exercises

1 Answer the questions.

Q1. Why are interracial marriages increasing?

Q2. Why do interracial couples have a very high level of acceptance?

Q3. Why do interracial couples never run out of topics to talk about?

Q4. Why would some interracial couples have different ways to bring up their children?

Q5. Which opportunity can interracial couples have?

2 Fill up the blanks using the words below.

interracial *drawback* *globalization* *charm* *involve*

1. ………..…………… has changed people's attitude all around the world.
2. Your fashion style is a part of your …………………… .
3. It is my …………………… , but also my advantage.
4. Do not …………………… me in this situation, I am indifferent.
5. We are an …………………… couple. I am from South Korea and she is from Japan.

3 Match the phrases to those given below.

1. Interracial couples do not give importance to skin color, tribe, or religion.
2. Interracial marriages often create unique and beautiful children.
3. Biracial children may face high level of discrimination.
4. Families of the interracial couples may have trouble interacting with each other.

a. They have language barriers.

b. Some people may criticize, taunt, and bully them.

c. If a strong relationship exists between them.

d. The children may inherit the best features of both parents.

4 Summary

Fill the blanks up using the words given below and complete the summary.

spouse, topics, discrimination, parenting, tribe, excitement, challenges

Interracial marriage is a marriage outside a social group, community, or ______________. It has lots of ______________ and charm, but at the same time, there are some ______________ and drawbacks for interracial couples. They have a high level of acceptance towards their ______________'s culture, values, and beliefs. Also, they never run out of ______________ to talk about and often have unique and beautiful children. On the other hand, biracial children face high level of ______________, stigma, and lack of acceptance from the society. ______________ styles also could be a problem of the couples. To sum up, it is important for interracial couples to compromise.

5 Find the mistake in each sentence and correct it by reshaping the underlined words.

1. Some people may even harm them physical.
2. Interracial marriages is a grow trend.
3. It is important to interracial couples to compromise.
4. Families may having trouble interacting with each other.
5. There are lots of challenges and hardships for both individuals involve.

6 Discussion Questions

1. Would you consider marrying a person from a different country?
2. Do you think interracial marriages will keep increasing?
3. Imagine you are a child from an interracial couple, how do you feel?
4. Why do some people hate biracial children?
5. Think of at least five elements that contribute for a successful interracial marriage.

7 Writing Time

Imagine if your child wants to marry a foreigner. Will you agree or disagree? Provide reasons and examples to support your opinion.

Unit 10

Is Capital Punishment Inevitable?

Warm Up Exercises

01 Answer these questions.

1. What does it mean by 'capital punishment'?
2. Does South Korea practice capital punishment?
3. Name 3 countries which practice capital punishment?

02 Put the words in right column.

Punishment, Victim, Criminal, Acquit, Ex-convict, Not guilty

Guilty	Innocent

Pre-Vocabulary Exercises

1 Match the words to their similar meaning.

1. Murderer	**a.** reduce
2. Commit	**b.** hinder
3. Curtail	**c.** killer
4. Atrocious	**d.** do
5. Deter	**e.** guiltless
6. Barbaric	**f.** awful
7. Innocent	**g.** savage

2 Find the meaning of the following phrases.

1. Legal process ____________________

2. Serious crime ____________________

3. Deal with ____________________

4. Engage in ____________________

Is Capital Punishment Inevitable?

Capital punishment, also known as death penalty is a legal process whereby the government executes a murderer for committing a serious crime. Capital punishment is still being practiced in some countries while most have abolished the death penalty. It may not be one of the most ideal choices for dealing with the criminals, however, it may curtail the occurrence of atrocious crimes. To be specific, many people believe that this functions as a deterrent to others so that they will learn a lesson and no longer engage in such abhorrent behavior. Capital punishment has been a controversial issue for a long time in many societies because of the various social and moral issues related to it.

Proponents of capital punishment claim that it has a significant impact to deter crimes. Firstly, capital punishment reduces crime rates by preventing the murderer from repeating the same act of violence. This is based on the philosophy of 'doing a small harm to prevent a greater harm'. Just as removing an infected part of a body is part a doctor's job because it will save patients' lives; eliminating criminals from society will save lives too. Unfortunately, criminals who commit crimes like murder, rape, or assault have no respect for human life. Therefore, they need to be brought to justice to face the punishments they rightfully deserve. Secondly, murderers and other prisoner who have committed extreme crimes are a serious threat to inmates. They can harm other prisoners. In addition, this also triggers a huge debate that the taxes paid by the citizens shouldn't be spent on a criminal having a life sentence.

On the other hand, opponents of capital punishment argue that it is inhumane and barbaric. Firstly, innocent people may be wrongly accused of killing and eventually executed in some cases. This violates the basic human rights everyone possesses.

In addition, some criminals suffer from mental illnesses that may have limited their judgment at the time of the crime. Secondly, the death penalty is a form of revenge that leaves little difference between the criminal and the law enforcing authorities. Furthermore, most criminals are poor and may not have the finances to seek help from powerful attorneys. This inability to pay for the services for their self-defense could mean a death sentence to them.

To sum up, With the contrasting views presented by proponents and opponents of capital punishment, it is quite challenging to decide which group was able to prove a more logical perspective regarding the issue. Besides the usefulness of capital punishment to keep the society safe from criminals, it is true that lots of innocent people have been wrongly executed. This may cause citizens to lose their faith in justice system and the law. It is very important for the government to take the public's perspectives in account before making laws about capital punishment.

Main Exercises

1 Answer the questions.

Q1. Why has capital punishment been a controversial issue for a long time?

Q2. How can capital punishment reduce crime rate?

Q3. Which philosophy is 'eliminating criminals from society' based on?

Q4. Why are prisoners, who have committed extreme crimes, a serious threat to inmates?

Q5. Why are most criminals unable to avail of legal services?

2 Fill up the blanks using the words below.

curtailed	*barbaric*	*murderer*	*commit*	*atrocious*

1. There is an absolute proof that he is the ....
2. He decided to .... a crime.
3. My salary was ....because of my mistake.
4. Police are trying to arrest the ....criminal.
5. Killing animals is a ....behavior.

3 Match the phrases to those given below.

1. Capital punishment has been a controversial issue.
2. Capital punishment reduces crime rate.
3. This is like removing an infected part of a body.
4. Innocent people may be wrongly accused.

a. It prevents the murderer from repeating the same act of violence.

b. This violates the basic human rights everybody possesses.

c. Various social and moral issues are related to it.

d. It will save patients' lives.

4 Summary

Fill the blanks up using the words given below and complete the summary.

executes, crime, controversial, reduces, debate, wrongly, authorities

Capital punishment is a legal process where the government ________________ a murderer for committing a serious ________________. Capital punishment has been a ________________ issue for a long time because of the various issues related to it. Proponents of capital punishment claim that it ________________ crime rates by preventing the murderer. Moreover, they can harm other prisoners and also may triggers a huge ________________ that the taxes spent on them. However, opponents of capital punishment believe innocent people may be ________________ accused. Furthermore, it is a form of revenge that leaves little difference between the criminal and the law enforcing ________________. To sum up, it is very important for the government to take the public's perspectives in account about capital punishment.

5 Find the mistake in each sentence and correct it by reshaping the underlined words.

1. The government executes a murderer for commit a serious crime.
2. Capital punishment is still being practice in some countries.
3. Capital punishment reduces crime rates by prevent the murderer.
4. This is base on the philosophy.
5. Innocent people may be wrongly accuse.

6 Discussion Questions

1. What is the best way to deal with criminals in jail?
2. What is the alternative to death penalty?
3. Do you agree with capital punishment?
4. What is the best way to compensate innocent people who are wrongly accused?
5. How can the government take the public's perspectives in account when making laws?

7 Writing Time

Which is better, death penalty or life sentence? What are merits and demerits of each punishment? Provide reasons and examples to support your opinion.

Unit 11

Should Contact Lens Replace Glasses?

Warm Up Exercises

01 **Answer these questions.**

1. What is a contact lens?
2. Do you wear glasses?
3. Have you ever used contact lenses?

02 **Put the words in right column.**

Frame, Tiny, Glass, Single-use, Thicker, Softer, Lighter,

Contact lens	Glasses

Pre-Vocabulary Exercises

1 Match the words to their similar meaning.

1. Organ	**a.** arrangement
2. Replacement	**b.** epidemic
3. Infection	**c.** a part of body
4. Superior	**d.** fit
5. Adjustment	**e.** better
6. Consult	**f.** counsel
7. Suit	**g.** substitute

2 Find the meaning of the following phrases.

1. Vision correction ________________________________

2. Fog up ________________________________

3. Keep in mind ________________________________

4. Fashion reason ________________________________

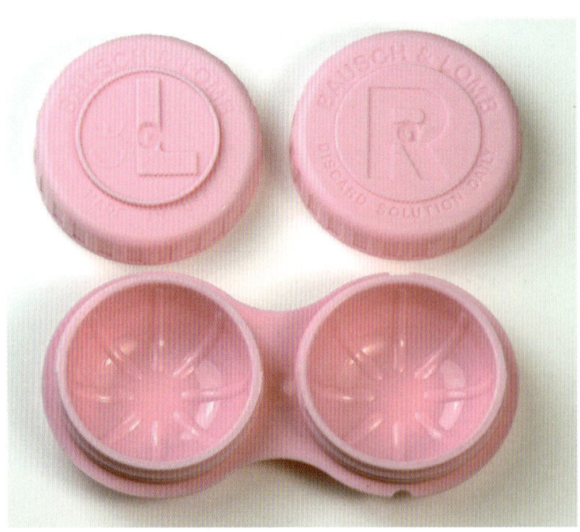

Should Contact Lens Replace Glasses?

Eyes are probably one of the most important and most beautiful organs in the human body. Most people constantly think about how to make themselves look more attractive. Especially, people who need to wear glasses for vision correction constantly think about whether to wear glasses or contact lenses. Eyeglasses are traditional tools for vision correction which are considered easier to clean, cheaper, and safer for the eyes. On the other hand, in the past few decades contact lenses have gained popularity and are considered a more modern and reliable replacement for eyeglasses. People wear them for both vision correction and fashion reasons. With the rapid developments in the contact lens industry and the advantages associated with them, it is quite difficult for most people to decide between eyeglasses or contact lens. Which do you prefer?

Proponents of eyeglasses consider them to be a more reliable and safer way to correct vision. Firstly, eyeglasses are more accurate for vision correction and are easy to use for people of all ages. Eyeglasses do not increase the risk to our eyes for an infection. Furthermore, they protect the eyes from getting hurt by dusty wind or any small particles flying in the air. Secondly, glasses are generally cheaper and easier to take care of compared to contact lenses that require frequent cleaning and moisturizing for better results. In addition, contact lenses need to be replaced quite often which costs a lot of money. Even though, some people may think glasses make them look silly, it is a trend nowadays to wear glasses to look more attractive. Celebrities who use glasses for fashion purposes include Emma Watson, Elton John, Tina Fey, and more.

Opponents of eyeglasses claim that they are an outdated item for vision correction;

therefore, contact lenses are the superior choice. Firstly, contact lenses can be used in any situation. For example, people who play sports may not feel comfortable wearing eyeglasses; therefore, contact lenses provide the safest solution. Another advantage of contact lenses is that they never fog up. Secondly, contact lenses are one of the fashion items that can provide people lots of confidence. Also, long term use of glasses can leave a permanent mark on nose that looks unpleasant. Furthermore, contact lenses are less distracting and do not require any adjustment like eyeglasses.

In conclusion, choosing to wear contact lenses or eyeglasses for vision correction mostly depends on people's lifestyles, comfort, and convenience. The important thing to keep in mind is that neither one is necessarily better than the other. Both have advantages and disadvantages. Therefore, the best way to make the decision is to consult an expert about what suits you most both physically and medically. So, which is better for your particular needs and lifestyle — glasses or contact lenses?

Main Exercises

1 Answer the questions.

Q1. What care do contact lenses need while they are being used?

Q2. Which celebrities use glasses for fashion purposes?

Q3. How do glasses protect eyes?

Q4. What is the disadvantage of eyeglasses?

Q5. Why are contact lenses generally more expensive than eyeglasses?

2 Fill up the blanks using the words below.

infection *organ* *superior* *replacement* *adjustments*

1. Eyes are the most beautiful ……………………in the human body.
2. I need a …………………… for my broken printer.
3. Good hygiene prevents the risk of …………………… .
4. 4G technology is ……………………to 3G.
5. We need some …………………… in our travel plan.

3 Match the phrases to those given below.

1. Contact lenses can be used in any situation.
2. Long term use of glasses can leave a permanent mark on nose.
3. Contact lenses need to be replaced quite often.
4. It is a trend nowadays to wear glasses to look more attractive.

a. It looks unpleasant.

b. People who play sports feel comfortable wearing contact lenses.

c. Even some celebrities use glasses for fashion reasons.

d. It costs a lot of money.

4 Summary

Fill the blanks up using the words given below and complete the summary.

popularity, decide, ages, rapid, expert, care, sports

In the past few decades contact lenses have gained ______________ and are considered a more modern and reliable replacement for eyeglasses. With ______________ developments in the contact lens industry and the advantages associated with them, it is quite difficult for most people to ______________ between eyeglasses or contact lens. Proponents of eyeglasses believe eyeglasses are more accurate for vision correction and are easy to use for people of all ______________ . Moreover, glasses are generally cheaper and easier to take ______________ of. On the other hand, opponents of eyeglasses prefer contact lenses because they can be used in any situation, even during playing ______________ . Secondly, contact lenses are one of the fashion items that can provide people lots of confidence since it doesn't disturb people's look. In conclusion, the best way to make the decision is to consult an ______________ about what suits you most both physically and medically.

5 Find the mistake in each sentence and correct it by reshaping the underlined words.

1. Choosing what to wear is depended on people's lifestyle, comfort, and convenience.
2. Eyeglasses are easy to using for people of all ages.
3. Glasses are generally cheaper and easier to take care of comparing to contact lenses
4. Contact lenses need to replace quite often which costs a lot of money.
5. People may think glasses make them looked silly.

6 Discussion Questions

1. Why does wearing contact lenses make people confident?
2. Name some celebrities who wear eyeglasses.
3. Why do more people in Korea wear eyeglasses compared to those in Europe?
4. What causes loss of vision?
5. How can people keep their eyes healthy?

7 Writing Time

Think of benefits and dangers of wearing contact lenses. Are they better than eyeglasses? Provide reasons and examples to support your opinion.

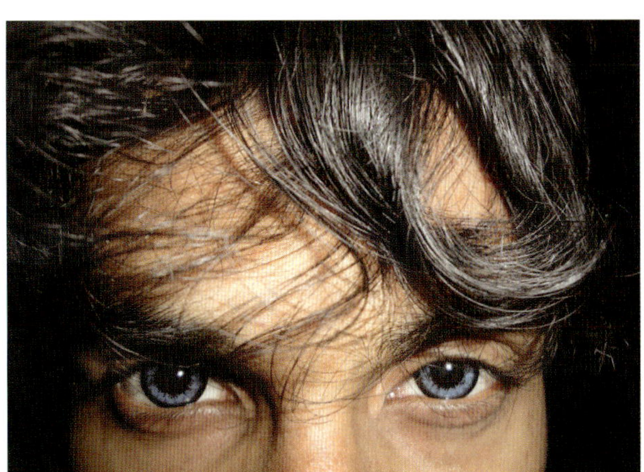

Unit 12
Are Superhero Movies Distractors?

Warm Up Exercises

01 **Answer these questions.**

1. Name at least 3 superhero movies that you have seen.
2. What is your favorite superhero movie?
3. Which superpower do you want to have?

02 **Put the words in right column.**

Paper, Video, Old-fashioned, Digital, Theater, TV, Drawing

Movie	Comic book

Pre-Vocabulary Exercises

1 Match the words to their similar meaning.

1. Stir	**a.** attract
2. Unity	**b.** sympathy
3. Impress	**c.** integration
4. Compassion	**d.** agitate
5. Dignity	**e.** invulnerable
6. Invincible	**f.** inspire
7. Fascinate	**g.** nobility

2 Find the meaning of the following phrases.

1. Indulge in ________________________

2. Strong moral ________________________

3. Forward thinkers ________________________

4. Supernatural power ________________________

Are Superhero Movies Distractors?

Can you name any five superhero movies that you have watched in past two years? Movies have been a source of entertainment and relaxation for a long time. From the moment people indulge in watching a movie, they are transformed into a new world where they see everything differently. Superhero movies are generally based on comic books that stir people's imagination. Superhero movies are considered to attract a wide range of audiences especially young people. Many people believe that superhero movies distract the audience because of their unrealistic themes, whereas others believe that they are a great way to think critically.

Proponents of superhero movies consider them a great source of entertainment. Firstly, superhero movies show a high level of unity and friendship. They present a great example of compassion, helpfulness, and dignity. The heroes in the movies impress their audience through their strong moral characters and invincible beliefs. Secondly, an outstanding demonstration of high technology animation is one of the main features of superhero movies. These movies are not only entertaining, but also a great way to introduce new ideas regarding future inventions. Young people get lots of innovative concepts that can help them to become more creative and forward thinkers. Furthermore, most superhero movies gain lots of business these days that helps to support all the people associated with it.

On the other hand, opponents of superhero movies claim that they are distractors especially to young people. Firstly, superhero movies divert young people's focus due to their unrealistic themes. Most movies are centered around a superhero that has supernatural powers which are used to overcome difficulties and to meet challenges. Secondly, over-reliance on technology and computer graphics exaggerate situations that can push the audience into a fantasy world. Vivid computer generated images and unrealistic characters can cause people to blur the lines between reality and fantasy. In addition, the predictable nature of most superhero movies, that the hero will definitely win, causes boredom for some people.

To sum up, superhero movies have both beneficial and harmful effects that mostly depend on what perspective an audience has while watching them. On a positive side, superhero movies offer a wide spectrum of events to the audience. They are full of the latest innovations and technology to fascinate the audience. On the other hand, the drawbacks of superhero movies including over reliance on technology, unrealistic images of characters, and predictable plots may make some audience members feel dissatisfied about their quality. The most important thing that people need while watching a superhero movie is a realistic approach. A realistic approach may help people to understand that the events and the characters are designed only for fantasy and to entertain audience rather than giving people false perspectives about life.

Main Exercises

1 Answer the questions.

Q1. Why do superhero movies divert young people's focus?

Q2. What can over-reliance on technology and computer graphics cause?

Q3. Which feature of most superhero movies can cause boredom for some people?

Q4. What can cause people to blur the lines between reality and fantasy?

Q5. What are superhero movies based on?

2 Fill up the blanks using the words below.

unity *compassion* *stir* *invincible* *impressed*

1. The leaves .... in the wind.
2. The world wants .... between the two Koreas.
3. The movie .... me a lot since it was very touching.
4. I felt .... for the tragedy.
5. No one can defeat him, he is ....

3 Match the phrases to those given below.

1. Superhero movies attract a wide range of audiences.
2. Superhero movies show a high level of unity and friendship.
3. High technology animation is one of the main features of superhero movies.
4. Computer generates unrealistic images and characters.

a. They present a great example of compassion, help, and dignity.

b. It can cause people to blur the lines between reality and fantasy.

c. They introduce new ideas regarding future inventions.

d. They are especially for young people.

4 Summary

Fill the blanks up using the words given below and complete the summary.

attract, friendship, technology, divert, graphics, approach, show

Superhero movies are considered to ________________ a wide range of audiences and a great way to think critically. However, many people believe that superhero movies distract the audience. Proponents of superhero movies argue that they ________________a high level of unity and ________________ which present compassion, help, and dignity. Moreover, the high ________________ animation of the movie introduces new ideas regarding future inventions. On the flip side, opponents of superhero movies ________________ young people's focus due to their unrealistic themes. over-reliance on technology and computer ________________ also can push the audience into a fantasy world. To sum up, people need a realistic ________________ to understand that the events and the characters are designed only for fantasy and to entertain audience.

5 Find the mistake in each sentence and correct it by reshaping the underlined words.

1. Superhero movies are consider to attract a wide range of audiences.
2. These movies are very entertain.
3. The hero will definite win.
4. They are transform into a new world.
5. Superhero movies are generally base on comic books.

6 Discussion Questions

1. Who is the oldest superhero?
2. What is the charm of the superhero movies?
3. Who is the most popular superhero recently?
4. Who is your favorite superhero? why?
5. Create your own superhero. And share its appearance with your peers.

7 Writing Time

Why are superhero movies becoming very popular recently? Is this phenomenon good or not? What are pros and cons of superhero movies? Provide reasons and examples to support your opinion.

Unit 13 Are Branded Goods Preferable?

Warm Up Exercises

01 Answer these questions.

1. Name 3 shoe brands?
2. Name at least 3 car brands.
3. What is your favorite computer brand?

02 Put the words in right column.

Department store, Expensive, Inexpensive, Flea market, High quality, Low quality

Branded goods	Unbranded goods

Pre-Vocabulary Exercises

1 Match the words to their similar meaning.

1. Obvious	**a.** taunt
2. Extra	**b.** lasting
3. Burden	**c.** expensive
4. Durable	**d.** definite
5. Reliable	**e.** additional
6. Bully	**f.** credible
7. Overpriced	**g.** load

2 Find the meaning of the following phrases.

1. Long-standing ______________________________

2. Getting damaged ______________________________

3. Social class ______________________________

4. Sense of belonging ______________________________

Are Branded Goods Preferable?

Goods that are identifiable as being the product of a particular manufacturer are called a brand. In other words, a brand is a name given to a product or service that is recognized by the public. There is a long-standing debate in many societies whether to buy branded goods or unbranded products. Of course, the most obvious difference between branded and unbranded is the price. Many people think branded goods are better because they may last longer; whereas, others claim that branded goods put extra burden to customers and usually have the same features as the unbranded products. What do you think?

Proponents of branded goods claim that branded products are more durable and reliable. Firstly, they can be used for a long period of time without any worries of getting damaged. In case any damage occurs, most companies provide customer service and reasonable exchange policies to their shoppers. In addition, branded good are mostly very attractive, comfortable, and innovative which gives the users a feeling of satisfaction about their purchase. Secondly, in most societies, branded goods define people's social class. It allows people to feel a sense of belonging in a certain social circle. In some cultures, bullying occurs because of the use of substandard goods. Furthermore, besides the fact that branded goods are comparatively more expensive than that of unbranded products, most stores offer coupons for future shopping.

Opponents of buying branded good argue that buying overpriced items is unreasonable. Firstly, in most cases, branded goods are of similar quality to non-branded goods. The companies charge extra money only to attach their brand name. In addition, this may cause extra financial burden to most families. Secondly, unbranded goods are accessible to almost every common citizen. Being human, it is very common to feel bored using the same clothes or shoes for a long time. Therefore, buying new ones feels like giving oneself a treat every now and then. Secondly, the craze to buy branded goods is truly harmful for the society as it breeds distinction among citizens. Brands are often blamed for creating a divide in society that widens the differences between the rich and the poor. Furthermore, unbranded goods offer access to any person in society to buy all necessities of daily life.

To sum up, buying branded or unbranded goods is a complicated issue that has no clear answer. People who like branded items find a way to buy them. On the other hand, those who do not like branded items or cannot afford them, mostly think it unreasonable to pay so much money for costly items. As it is mentioned above, branded items are sometimes blamed for social divisions, therefore, it is important to maintain a balance between branded and unbranded goods to protect both groups' self-esteem and desires.

Main Exercises

1 Answer the questions.

Q1. What is the main difference between branded and unbranded items?

Q2. Why can branded goods be used for a long period of time?

Q3. Why is the craze to buy branded goods harmful for society?

Q4. How does bullying occur in some cultures regarding purchasing goods?

Q5. Why are branded goods more expensive than non-branded goods?

2 Fill up the blanks using the words below.

obvious *bully* *burden* *durable* *extra*

1. It is .... that Jack did it because he was there.

2. There is an .... charge for more service.

3. The .... was too heavy to carry.

4. Those chairs are ...., so they last long.

5. Do not .... your friend or you will be punished.

3 Match the phrases to those given below.

1. Brands are often blamed for creating a divide in society.

2. Branded good are mostly very attractive, comfortable, and innovative.

3. Branded goods define people's social class.

4. Unbranded goods are in access to almost every common citizen.

a. People can easily buy cheaper goods that they need.

b. It widens the differences between the rich and the poor.

c. It gives the users a feeling of satisfaction about their purchase.

d. It allows people to feel a sense of belonging in a certain social circle.

4 Summary

Fill the blanks up using the words given below and complete the summary.

charge, period, similar, access, service, while, circle

A brand is a name given to a product or service that is recognized by the public. Many people think branded goods are better ________________ others claim that branded goods put extra burden to customers. Proponents of branded goods believe that they can be used for a long ________________ of time with customer ________________ and exchange policies. Moreover, it allows people to feel a sense of belonging in a certain social ________________. Opponents of buying branded good argue that the companies ________________ extra money only to attach their brand name though both have ________________ quality. Also, unbranded goods are in ________________ to almost every common citizen. To sum up, it is important to maintain a balance between branded and unbranded goods to protect both groups' self-esteem and desires.

5 Find the mistake in each sentence and correct it by reshaping the underlined words.

1. A brand is a name giving to a product.
2. They can be using for a long period.
3. Bullying is occure because of the use of substandard goods.
4. Buying branded or unbranded goods are a complicated issue.
5. There is a long-standing debate whether for buy branded goods.

6 Discussion Questions

1. When do you want to buy branded goods?
2. What is the most expensive item that you have? Describe it.
3. Which brand do you like the most? why?
4. Which country produces the most brands?
5. Where do you get non-branded goods?

7 Writing Time

Why do people like branded goods? Do you prefer branded goods over non-branded goods? Provide reasons and examples to support your opinion.

Unit 14

Is Fortune Telling Helpful?

Warm Up Exercises

01 Answer these questions.

1. What is fortune telling?
2. Do you believe in fortune telling?
3. Guess how to become a fortune teller.

02 Put the words in right column.

Vague, Accurate, Ancient, Causality, Dream, Scientist, Shaman

Superstition	Science

Pre-Vocabulary Exercises

1 Match the words to their similar meaning.

1. Method	**a.** forecast
2. Harsh	**b.** block
3. Forthcoming	**c.** way
4. Prediction	**d.** gaze
5. Exert	**e.** cruel
6. Stare	**f.** exercise
7. Deadlock	**g.** approaching

2 Find the meaning of the following phrases.

1. Eager to ______________________

2. Deal with ______________________

3. False hope ______________________

4. Cup of tea ______________________

Is Fortune Telling Helpful?

Are you superstitious? Do you believe that fortune tellers can predict future events? Fortune tellers use various methods including looking at a client's palm, birth year, date of birth, and / or facial expressions. The most popular method, however, is through cards. There are usually both pros and cons about everything in life. Many people are eager to know something interesting about their future. It's extremely difficult to deal with uncertainty and face unknown events. Harsh realities of life and different challenges make us turn to fortune tellers in order to get a good advice. Some people believe that fortune tellers often cheat people out of their money, while others believe that they can be a great life guide and give desperate people motivation.

Proponents of fortune tellers claim that they tell people about possible forthcoming hardships in their lives so they can prepare to face them. Firstly, getting advice from a fortune teller guides people in a proper and safe direction. If there is a prediction about an accident in the future, people can avoid them by being more cautious. Secondly, most people find it interesting and exciting to know about the future events that may occur in their lives. These predictions sometimes help people decide about their marriage partners or starting new businesses. It may help them to save a lot of time worrying about whether to decide or not.

Opponents of fortune tellers argue that their words can exert huge negative influences on the lives of brilliant people. Firstly, fortune tellers fill people's minds with unrealistic ideas, false hopes, and fear. Psychologists say that fortune telling can seriously damage your mental well-being. Highly successful and happy people rarely visit fortune tellers, because it's not their cup of tea. They are the ones who know what they want and how to turn their dreams into reality. Secondly, fortune telling may break existing relationships. When people hear the fortune tellers saying that they have some enemy around them, they start staring at everyone in suspicious ways. That look may offend many friends, relatives, or coworkers and consequently, the relationships may turn bad.

In conclusion, at first sight, fortune telling seems like a very interesting and captivating process. Some people certainly take advantage of it and find them helpful. On the other hand, others consider their visits to fortune tellers a nightmare. They start losing faith in their abilities and become emotionally weak after these visits. They believe that it is the best way to secure their future. One alternative to avoid going to fortune tellers is to ask wise and experienced people for a valuable advice. In most cases, they know how to break the deadlock and help people deal with despair.

Main Exercises

1 Answer the questions.

Q1. What is the fortune teller's most popular method?

Q2. Why are many people eager to know their future?

Q3. Why do highly successful and happy people rarely visit fortune tellers?

Q4. Why can fortune telling break existing relationships.

Q5. What is one alternative to avoid going to fortune tellers?

2 Fill up the blanks using the words below.

prediction　　*method*　　*harsh*　　*stare*　　*forthcoming*

1. Let's use the 2nd..................sincethefirstonefailed.
2. It is .... that some people die of hunger.
3. The .... law will change a lot.
4. The .... of the weather agency was wrong.
5. Why do you .... at me? Is there something on my face?

3 Match the phrases to those given below.

1. There are harsh realities of life and different challenges.
2. Fortune tellers tell people about possible forthcoming hardships.
3. Predictions sometimes help people decide about making a decision.
4. People may hear the fortune tellers saying that they have some enemies around them.

a. They start staring at everyone in suspicious ways.

b. It makes us turn to fortune tellers in order to get a good advice.

c. It may help them to save a lot of time worrying about whether to decide or not.

d. They can prepare to face them.

4 Summary

Fill the blanks up using the words given below and complete the summary.

break, turn, eager, it, avoid, direction, fill

Many people are ________________ to know something interesting about their future. Also, harsh realities of life and different challenges make us _________________ to fortune tellers in order to get a good advice. Proponents of fortune telling claim that fortune telling provides a right and safe ________________. Furthermore, most people find ________________ interesting and exciting to know about the future events. Opponents of fortune tellers insist that they ________________ people's minds with unrealistic ideas, false hopes, and fear. In addition, fortune telling sometimes can ________________ existing relationships. One alternative to ________________ going to fortune tellers is to ask wise and experienced people for a valuable advice.

5 Find the mistake in each sentence and correct it by reshaping the underlined words.

1. People can avoid them at changing their lives.
2. Most people find it interesting and exciting for know about the future events.
3. It may help them to save a lot of time worrying about if to decide and not.
4. Fortune tellers fill people's minds by unrealistic ideas.
5. Fortune telling is seemed like a very interesting process.

6 Discussion Questions

1. Is life predetermined? Why or why not?
2. Have you ever visited a fortune teller? Why or why not?
3. Where can you meet a fortune teller?
4. Are fortune tellers credible? Why or why not?
5. What is your own way to predict the future?

7 Writing Time

Do you believe in fortune telling or any other superstitions? What are pros and cons of visiting fortune tellers? Provide reasons and examples to support your opinion.

Unit 15 Do Celebrities Need Privacy?

Warm Up Exercises

01 **Answer these questions.**

1. What is a celebrity?
2. Name at least 3 most popular celebrities.
3. Who is your favorite celebrity?

02 **Put the words in right column.**

Drama, Office, Actor, Famous, Paparazzi, Normal, Salary

Celebrities	Ordinary people

Pre-Vocabulary Exercises

1 Match the words to their similar meaning.

1. Possess	**a.** amusement
2. Invasion	**b.** Friendly
3. Entertainment	**c.** attack
4. Lavish	**d.** own
5. Intimate	**e.** chore
6. Stalk	**f.** track
7. Errand	**g.** luxurious

2 Find the meaning of the following phrases.

1. Taking a closer look ______________________

2. Turn into ______________________

3. Giving up ______________________

4. In terms of ______________________

Do Celebrities Need Privacy?

A celebrity is a person who is widely recognized in a society and attracts a fair amount of public and media attention. Celebrities are a part of each culture that provide entertainment to the public. In the modern age, fans of celebrities often look for opportunities to take a closer look into their favorite artist's life. In some cases, their love and passion for their favorite stars can turn into an obsession that drives them to know all of the intimate secrets of their lives. This obsession with celebrities can cause a huge amount of stress for some artists and they consider it an invasion of their private lives. Most people think that the celebrities have a right to protect their privacy. However, others claim that celebrities are public figures and that this is their choice to become famous by giving up their privacy.

Proponents of a celebrity's right to privacy claim that artists are human beings like everyone else and as such they possess the right to live their lives peacefully. As humans they need to be able to take care of their daily errands like grocery shopping, cleaning their houses, cooking, etc. If they are not given any privacy, their lives will be badly limited. In addition, this invasion of their privacy can hurt their families too. Their children may not be able to enjoy spending time with their friends or playing outside of their houses. Secondly, celebrities are entertainers who possess a special talent which provides a public good entertainment. In order to pursue their careers, they need to practice their skills in privacy. A constant chase by the paparazzi could disrupt their effort to develop their skills. Furthermore, celebrities provide entertainment to the public and that brings joy to society and may even cause a reduction in crime. It is possible that this celebrity stalking could cause some people to feel hesitation to choose to seek future fame.

In contrast, people who think celebrity's lives should be visible to the public argue that celebrities are well aware of the nature of their jobs as public figures. Firstly, they choose the path of fame; and fans' love and devotion for them can be even a draw to a life of fame. Many celebrities may even enjoy being chased and being photographed. In addition, a TV star's life requires a spotlight. The moment celebrities lose the public's attention they are forgotten by the fans and their career could be over. Secondly, it is the fans who finance the leisure and lavish lifestyles that celebrities enjoy. An abdication of personal privacy is just a small cost of enjoying the life of luxury.

In conclusion, even though celebrities make an informed decision to be public figures, they should retain their rights to enjoy a private life with their family and friends without any outside interruption. Celebrities contribute to the society in terms of providing the public entertainment. This helps a nation and its citizens to become united and feel pride. Celebrities privacy protection laws should be made with the consent of both the government and the public that could provide celebrities a chance to enjoy their lives peacefully.

Main Exercises

1 Answer the questions.

Q1. How can fan's invasion of privacy hurt stars' families?

Q2. What happens if a celebrity loses the public's attention?

Q3. How can stars pursue their careers?

Q4. Why could many celebrities enjoy being chased and being photographed?

Q5. Who finances the leisure and lavish lifestyles that celebrities enjoy?

2 Fill up the blanks using the words below.

invasion *entertainment* *possess* *stalk* *intimate*

1. Celebrities work for ………………...…industry.
2. We are ………………...…friends.
3. The movie is about alien ………………...…of Earth.
4. I want to ………………...…the building where I live.
5. The detective is going to ………………...…the suspect of the case.

3 Match the phrases to those given below.

1. Fan love their stars.
2. Celebrities need to practice their skills in privacy.
3. Celebrities are well aware of the nature of their jobs as public figures.
4. Celebrities contribute to the society in terms of providing the public entertainment.

a. Many celebrities may even enjoy being chased and being photographed.
b. It is to pursue their careers.
c. Their love can turn into an obsession sometimes.
d. This helps a nation and its citizens to become united and feel pride.

4 Summary

Fill the blanks up using the words given below and complete the summary.

privacy, attention, figures, society, path, skills, enjoy

A celebrity is a person who is widely recognized in a _______________ and attracts a fair amount of public and media _______________. Most people think that the celebrities have a right to protect their privacy while others claim that celebrities are public _______________ and that this is their choice to become famous by giving up their privacy. Proponents of celebrity's rights to _______________ claim that they need to be able to take care of their daily errands since they are same human beings. Moreover, they need to practice their _______________ in privacy in order to pursue their careers. On the other hand, opponents of celebrity's rights to privacy insist that they choose the _______________ of fame. Secondly, it is the fans who finance the leisure and lavish lifestyles that celebrities _______________. To sum up, celebrities should retain their rights to enjoy a private life so celebrities' privacy protection laws should be made.

5 Find the mistake in each sentence and correct it by reshaping the underlined words.

1. Fans often look at the opportunities to take a closer look into their favorite artist's life.
2. Most people think that the celebrities have a right for protect their privacy.
3. Celebrities privacy protection laws should be make.
4. This is their choice to become famous by give up their privacy.
5. If they are not given any privacy, their lives will be badly limit.

6 Discussion Questions

1. Who is the most famous celebrity in Korea?
2. Is being a star always wonderful? Why or why not?
3. Do you know any star affected by a fan?
4. Why do fans want to know about their stars' private life?
5. Are there paparazzi in Korea?

7 Writing Time

Imagine you are a popular celebrity. Which merits and demerits of being a celebrity can you have? Provide reasons and examples to support your opinion.

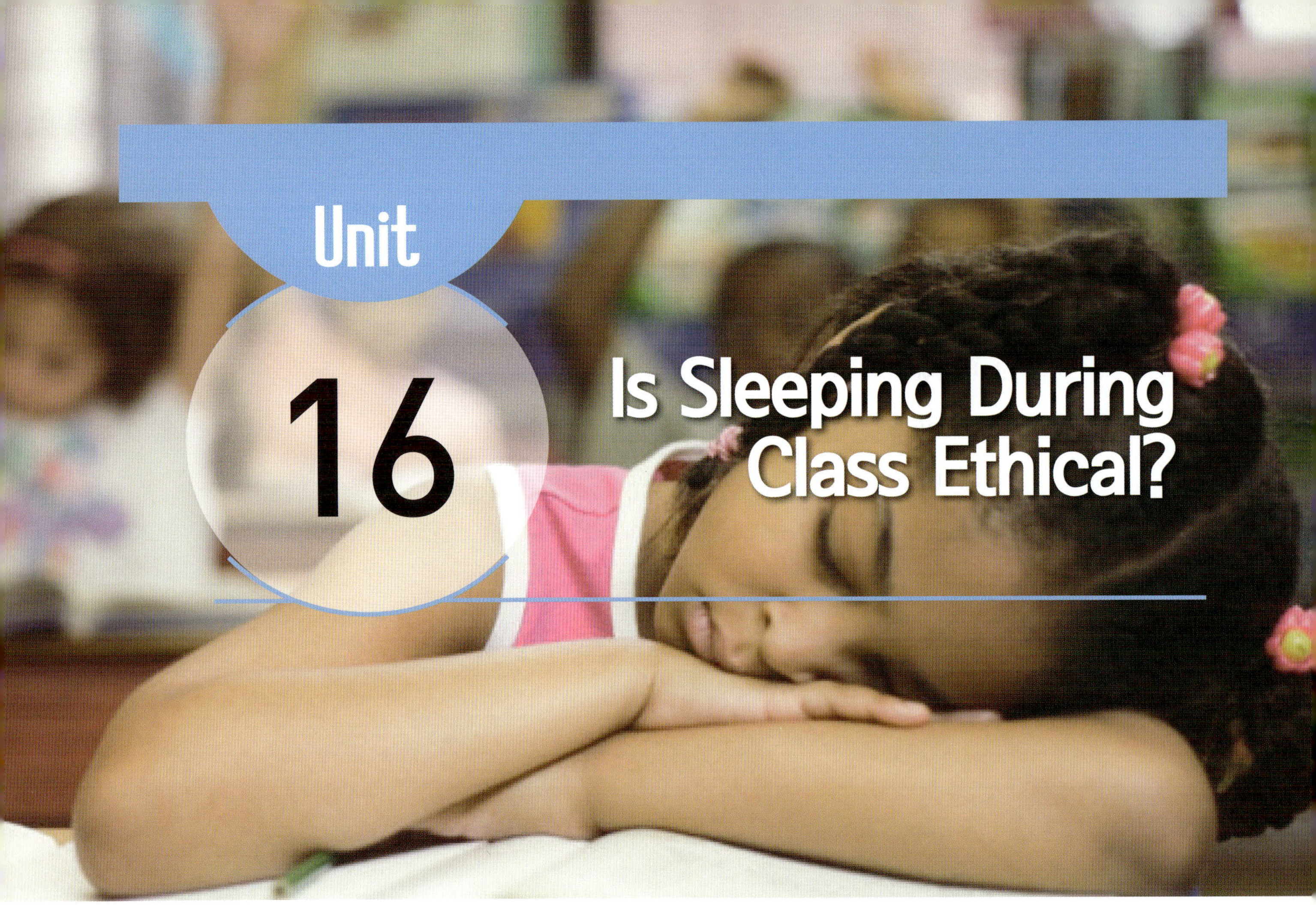

Unit 16 Is Sleeping During Class Ethical?

Warm Up Exercises

01 **Answer these questions.**

1. What does it mean by a nap?
2. Do you take a nap during the daytime?
3. Have you ever fallen asleep during class?

02 **Put the words in right column.**

Long, Short, Pajamas, Daytime, Doze, Night

Nap	Sleep at night

Pre-Vocabulary Exercises

1 Match the words to their similar meaning.

1. Ventilation	a. disregard
2. Extracurricular	b. recharge
3. Sufficient	c. air circulation
4. Inappropriate	d. short sleep
5. Disrespect	e. enough
6. Refresh	f. additional
7. Nap	g. improper

2 Find the meaning of the following phrases.

1. Stay up ______________________
2. Following day ______________________
3. Switch off ______________________
4. Taking a nap ______________________

Is Sleeping During Class Ethical?

Have you ever fallen asleep during class? Most people may have had this experience at least once in their life. There are many factors that cause students to sleep during class including having big meals before class, a lack of sleep, or even poor ventilation. Many people think that a short nap during class offers many benefits including a refreshed feeling, feeling more ready to learn, and a positive attitude. On the other hand, some consider taking a nap during class time to be harmful for the student and the class. Do you think taking short naps in class is harmful for students?

Proponents of sleeping during class insist that it offers many health and educational benefits. Firstly, taking a nap during class helps students to concentrate on rest of the lesson well. Some students stay up late at night and take many classes the following day which is naturally exhausting. A short nap helps them feel active and fresh for rest of the day. In addition, students are more productive after taking a short nap than struggling to stay awake. Secondly, studies claim that a short nap after some learning is the best way to remember new information. This enhances students' capability to memorize information in a short time.

Opponents of sleeping during class argue that students go to school to learn and sleeping during class negatively affects their progress and learning. Firstly, school is a place to learn and students go to school to engage in the learning process and that requires effort and determination. Falling asleep during class wastes their precious time. Secondly, sleeping in class might send the teacher and other students the wrong message. Some people may think it is rude to sleep when someone is teaching. In addition, sleeping in class will set a bad example for the other students that will create harm to the learning environment. Furthermore, sleeping in class may develop the bad habit of sleeping during important tasks in the future life.

In conclusion, students sleep in class due to the extra burden of homework, assignments, extracurricular activities, and lack of sufficient sleep time at night. However, opponents of sleeping in class consider it inappropriate to sleep during class. They think sleeping affects the whole class atmosphere and shows disrespect to the teacher. In order to avoid sleeping during class, students may need to reduce their extra activities during the semester time in order to have enough sleep at night. In addition, if they switch off their digital devices and go to bed earlier, they will feel fresher the next morning and will not feel sleepy during class. Furthermore, students, who are feeling very sleepy, may leave class and find some quiet spot outside of classroom to take a nap. This will prevent any negative effect on the class atmosphere.

Main Exercises

1 Answer the questions.

Q1. What makes students feel sleepy during class?

Q2. What is the best way to remember new information?

Q3. How can sleeping in class develop into a bad habit?

Q4. How can sleeping in class be prevented?

Q5. What should students do when they feel very sleepy?

2 Fill up the blanks using the words below.

disrespect *nap* *inappropriate* *sufficient* *refresh*

1. Teenagers need ....sleep to grow taller.
2. This medicine may be ....for children under 10.
3. He always shows ....to the elderly, he is rude.
4. I take a walk along the river to ....myself.
5. I always take a ....after lunch.

3 Match the phrases to those given below.

1. A short nap after some learning helps to remember new information.
2. If they switch off their digital devices at night,
3. Some students stay up late at night and take many classes the following day.
4. Students go to school to engage in the learning process.

a. They will be exhausted.

b. This helps to memorize information in a short time.

c. They will feel fresher the next morning.

d. It requires effort and determination.

4 Summary

Fill the blanks up using the words given below and complete the summary.

extra, way, student, teaching, falling, concentrate

Many people think that a short nap during class offers many benefits. However, others consider that taking a nap during class time is harmful for the ____________ and the class. Proponents of sleeping during class insist that taking a nap during class helps students to ____________ on rest of the lesson well. Secondly, studies claim that a short nap after some learning is the best ____________ to remember new information. Opponents of sleeping during class argue that school is a place to learn and ____________ asleep during class merely wastes their precious time. Moreover, some people may think it is rude to sleep when someone is ____________ . To sum up, in order to avoid sleeping during class, students may need to reduce their ____________ activities during the semester time in order to have enough sleep at night.

5 Find the mistake in each sentence and correct it by reshaping the underlined words.

1. Taking a nap during class helps students to concentrate out rest of the lesson well.
2. This enhances students' capable to memorize information.
3. Sleeping in class will be set a bad example for the other students.
4. A short nap helps them feel actively.
5. Sleeping in class might send to the teacher and other students the wrong message.

6 Discussion Questions

1. Have you ever fallen asleep during class?
2. What makes you sleepy during class?
3. How can teachers help students' learning?
4. Why do teachers hate students who sleep during class?
5. Is there any solution to prevent taking naps during class?

7 Writing Time

Should schools allow some nap time during class? Will it help students' learning? Provide reasons and examples to support your opinion.

| 저자약력 |

About the Author

Bilal Qureshi earned his Doctorate degree in TESOL at Queen's University Belfast, UK and currently teaches at Seokyeong University Seoul. He has been interested in variety of issues related to second language learners' motivation and skill development; and this series of books shows his dedication and passion toward this goal. Email: qureshi@skuniv.ac.kr

Acknowledgement

I want to thank everyone who helped me through this process especially the reviewer and proofreader Professor David Miller, whose hard work motivated me a lot. I also show my appreciation to Professor Uk Chang from Duksung Women's University, Zeeshan Qureshi, Kim Bora, Jeong MinGyu, Hwang Junsook, and above all, my mother whose constant encouragement helped me complete this project.

Progressive Debate Active 2

2019년 1월 20일 1판 1쇄 인쇄
2019년 1월 25일 1판 1쇄 발행

저 자 | BILAL QURESHI
발행인 | 이수영
발행처 | 도서출판 **청람**
서울시 마포구 독막로 288(대흥동, 세양상가 109호)
전 화 | 02)3272-2601~2
팩 스 | 02)3272-2603
이메일 | crbooks@daum.net
홈페이지 | http://www.crbooks.co.kr
등 록 | 2000.8.26. 제6-0509호

ISBN 978-89-5972-668-4 93740 [정가 13,000원]

Audio files:
www.crbooks.co.kr/progressiveActive2/